All you need to know about Turkey

Introduction

Turkey, a country with a rich history and a fascinating variety of landscapes, cultures, and traditions, is a captivating topic for anyone interested in the world and its different facets. Geographically, Turkey spans two continents, Europe and Asia, with most of the country located in the Middle East. Turkey is bordered by the Black Sea to the north, the Aegean Sea to the west and the Mediterranean Sea to the south. The neighboring countries are Greece and Bulgaria to the west, Georgia, Armenia, Azerbaijan and Iran to the east, and Syria and Iraq to the southeast. With an area of over 780,000 square kilometers, Turkey is larger than any other European country except Russia.

Turkey's history dates back a long way to ancient times, when the area was part of the Greek and later the Roman Empire. Later, it became the center of the mighty Byzantine Empire, which experienced its heyday in the Middle Ages. In the 13th century, the Ottomans conquered the country and founded the Ottoman Empire, which lasted until the beginning of the 20th century. After the First World War, Turkey signed the Treaty of Lausanne and became a modern republic in 1923, led by Mustafa Kemal Ataturk.

Today, Turkey is a multi-layered nation that combines both European and Oriental influences. The population of over 80 million people reflects this diversity, with the majority of the population of Turkish descent and Turkish being the official language of the country. In addition to Turkish, there are a number of minority languages spoken in certain regions, including Kurdish, Arabic, and various Caucasian languages.

Turkey has developed into a dynamic economic power based on agriculture, industry and tourism. Tourism plays a particularly important role, as the country offers a variety of historical landmarks, stunning coastal landscapes, and modern cities that attract visitors from all over the world. Some of the most famous sights include the Hagia Sophia and Topkapi Palace in Istanbul, the ancient ruins of Ephesus and Troy, the unique rock formations of Cappadocia, and the beautiful beaches of the Turkish Riviera.

Turkey's culture is characterized by a rich tradition of literature, music, crafts and architecture. Turkish cuisine is known worldwide for its variety and flavor, from spicy kebabs and meze appetizers to sweet baklava desserts. Religiously, Turkey is mainly Muslim, with Islam being the dominant religion, but with a strong tradition of religious freedom and a diversity of faiths.

In recent years, Turkey has experienced a number of social and political changes that have shaped the country and its role in the global arena. Despite challenges, Turkey remains a fascinating country that impresses visitors with its hospitality, history, and cultural diversity. In this book, we will dive deep into the different aspects of this country and offer a comprehensive insight into Turkey, its people, and its culture.

The Geography of Turkey

Turkey's geography is extremely diverse, ranging from breathtaking coastal landscapes to fertile plains and imposing mountain ranges. The country covers an area of more than 780,000 square kilometers and is mostly located in the Middle East, with a smaller part in southeastern Europe. Turkey borders the Black Sea in the north, whose coasts are characterized by steep cliffs and green forests. To the west stretches the Aegean Sea with its numerous islands and a mild Mediterranean climate ideal for growing olives and wine.

Along Turkey's southern coastline lies the Mediterranean Sea, with a variety of beaches, bays and historic cities such as Antalya and Alanya. The country's coastline is over 7,200 kilometers long in total, making Turkey one of the most diverse coastal countries in the world. To the east of the country, Iran stretches all the way to the Ararat Mountains, whose summit is the highest point in Turkey at over 5,100 meters and offers a breathtaking sight.

Turkey's landscapes are also characterized by various geological formations, including the Taurus Mountains in the south, which separates the coastal region from the central highlands. This highland, known as the Anatolian Plateau, is largely a fertile plain that stretches between mountain ranges and provides important agricultural land for the cultivation of grains, cotton, and other crops. In the northeast of the country stretch the green forests of the Pontic Mountains, which dominate the regions along the Black Sea.

Turkey is also home to a variety of bodies of water, including numerous rivers such as the Euphrates, the Tigris and the Sakarya, which supply the country with water and are of great importance for irrigation projects. In some regions, especially in the southeastern Anatolian region, the climate is dry and desert-like, while in other areas such as the coast and northeast, it is more temperate and humid.

Turkey's geopolitical location has made it an important crossroads between Europe and Asia, resulting in both cultural and economic influences. The capital Ankara is centrally located in Anatolia and is the political and administrative center of the country, while Istanbul, as the largest city in the country, plays a key role as a cultural and economic center.

Overall, Turkey's geography offers an impressive variety of landscapes, ranging from historic cities to majestic mountains and picturesque coastlines that attract visitors from all over the world, making the country a fascinating destination.

The History of Turkey: Ancient Times

Turkey's history dates back to ancient times, when the area was part of several significant civilizations that shaped the region's cultural and political heritage. Over 12,000 years ago, Anatolia began to be settled by various Neolithic cultures, traces of which can be found in archaeological finds such as Göbekli Tepe, one of the oldest temple complexes in the world.

In ancient times, Anatolia was a melting pot of cultures and peoples. Around 2000 BC, the Hittites settled in central Anatolia and established a significant empire with an advanced civilization known for its bronze art and cuneiform. They ruled over large parts of Anatolia and had significant trade relations with the neighboring peoples in the Middle East.

In the 7th century BC, the Lycians and Lydians settled in southwestern and western Turkey and founded their own independent kingdoms. Greek colonization began in the 8th century BC along the Aegean and Pontic coasts of Anatolia, giving rise to significant cities such as Miletus, Ephesus, and Byzantion (later known as Constantinople and Istanbul).

In the 6th century BC, the Persians under Cyrus II conquered Anatolia and integrated it into their powerful Achaemenid Empire, which stretched from Central Asia to the eastern Mediterranean. The Persians were later defeated by Alexander the Great in the 4th century BC, who took over the entire Persian Empire and ushered in the Hellenistic Age, which was a cultural heyday in Anatolia.

After Alexander's death, Anatolia was divided between the Diadochi, but the Hellenistic presence remained strong, especially among the Seleucids and the Ptolemies. The region eventually became part of the Roman Empire, which began to conquer and Romanize Anatolia from the 2nd century BC. Cities such as Ephesus and Pergamum flourished under Roman rule and became centers of trade, culture, and Christianity.

In the 4th century AD, Christianity became the dominant religion in Anatolia after Emperor Constantine the Great recognized Christianity as the state religion of the Roman Empire. The Byzantine Empire, which developed from the eastern part of the Roman Empire, took Anatolia as its core region and made Byzantium (later Constantinople) its capital.

The history of antiquity in Turkey is marked by a rich diversity of cultures, religions and political developments that have laid the foundation for modern Turkey. The remains of ancient cities, temples and works of art bear witness to the cultural and historical importance of Anatolia in ancient world history.

The History of Turkey: Byzantine Empire

The Byzantine Empire played a central role in Turkey's history and shaped the cultural, political and religious fabric of the region for centuries. After the division of the Roman Empire in 395 AD, the Eastern Roman Empire, known as the Byzantine Empire, took control of Anatolia and most of what is now Turkey. Constantinople (present-day Istanbul) became the capital of this new empire, which lasted for almost a millennium from 330 to 1453 AD.

Under Emperor Justinian I, who ruled from 527 to 565 AD, the Byzantine Empire reached its greatest extent and experienced a renaissance in art, architecture and law. The Hagia Sophia, one of the most important churches in Christendom, was built under his rule and still stands today as a testimony to the splendor of Byzantine architecture. The legal system of Roman law was codified and influenced many European legal systems.

The Byzantine Empire repeatedly fought against invasions and attacks from outside, including the Persians in the east and the Arabs in the 7th century, who weakened the empire but did not defeat it. In the 11th century, the empire experienced a short-term recovery under Emperor

Basil II and was able to reconquer large parts of Anatolia.

The religious landscape of Anatolia was strongly influenced by the Byzantine Empire. Orthodox Christianity became the dominant religion and Christianity was closely linked to the cultural identity of the empire. The Patriarch of Constantinople, as the supreme spiritual leader of Orthodox Christendom, had a great influence on religious life in the entire region.

The end of the Byzantine Empire came in 1453, when Ottoman troops under Sultan Mehmed II conquered Constantinople. This conquest marked the end of the Byzantine era and the beginning of the Ottoman Empire, which moved its capital to Istanbul and took control of Anatolia and large parts of southeastern Europe.

The history of the Byzantine Empire in Turkey left a legacy of architecture, art and religion that is still present today. Many of the Byzantine churches, monasteries and palaces were taken over by the Ottomans and continued to be used or converted into mosques. Byzantine art, especially icon painting and mosaic art, influenced Ottoman art, leaving behind a cultural exchange that has shaped the history of Turkey into the modern era.

The History of Turkey: Ottoman Empire

The Ottoman Empire, which existed from 1299 to 1922, marks one of the most significant periods in Turkey's history and shaped the political, cultural and social fabric of the region for centuries. Founded by Osman I, a Turkmen leader in northwestern Anatolia, the empire began as a small beylik that quickly expanded through conquest and diplomatic alliances.

In the 14th and 15th centuries, the Ottoman Empire conquered large parts of Anatolia and Balkan regions and expanded into southeastern Europe until the peak of its power under Sultan Suleiman the Magnificent in the 16th century. Under his rule, the empire encompassed a considerable part of southeastern Europe, the Middle East and North Africa, and parts of the Persian Gulf.

The Ottoman Empire was known for its tolerance of ethnic and religious minorities who lived under its protection and nurtured their own communities and institutions. Non-Muslims paid a special tax called protection money, but they had extensive religious freedoms and were allowed to have their own judicial systems and educational institutions.

The capital of the Ottoman Empire was Constantinople, which became the capital after the conquest by Sultan Mehmed II in 1453 and was later renamed Istanbul. Istanbul became not only the political and administrative center of the empire, but also the cultural and economic heart that controlled trade routes between East and West.

The Ottoman Empire was a multicultural empire inhabited by Turks, Arabs, Persians, Kurds, Greeks, Armenians, Jews, and many other ethnic and religious groups. The main religion of the empire was Sunni Islam, and the sultan was considered the political and religious leader of the Muslims in the empire. In addition to Islam, however, there were a variety of other religious groups that maintained their own traditions and practices.

Ottoman society was divided into different classes and professions, with the elite consisting of the sultan's ruling family and the high officials of the state. Ottoman military power was based on the discipline and organization of its armed forces, especially the Janissaries, an elite unit of slave-soldiers who were among the best fighters in the empire.

The Ottoman Empire experienced an economic decline in the 17th century due to internal corruption, economic stagnation and increasing European expansion. In the 19th century, the empire began to lose large parts of its territory to European powers, leading to a period of retreat and reforms under the Tanzimat Edict, which included modernization measures such as the introduction of a modern legal system and educational reforms.

The Ottoman Empire formally ended after World War I with the signing of the Treaty of Sèvres in 1920, which divided the empire into small independent states and greatly reduced its territory. The Republic of Turkey was founded in 1923 under the leadership of Mustafa Kemal Ataturk, who led the country through a period of modernization and secularization, with Istanbul continuing to function as the country's cultural and economic center.

The legacy of the Ottoman Empire in Turkey is still present today, especially in the architecture, language, art and traditions of Turkish society. It was an era of diversity and cultural exchange that made Turkey an intersection of civilizations and a bridge between East and West.

History of Turkey: Republic of Turkey

The founding of the Republic of Turkey in 1923 marked a crucial turning point in the country's history, heralding the end of the Ottoman era and the beginning of a modern, secular nation led by Mustafa Kemal Ataturk. Ataturk, a high-ranking officer of the Ottoman Empire and leader of the Turkish independence movement, led the successful defense against the occupying forces of World War I and negotiated the Treaty of Lausanne in 1923, which recognized Turkey's independence.

The Republic of Turkey was founded on the principles of secularism, national sovereignty, democracy and social justice. Ataturk carried out far-reaching reforms, including the introduction of the Latin alphabet to replace the Arabic script, the reform of the education system, the separation of religion and state, and the modernization of the legal system according to the Western model.

The capital was moved from Istanbul to Ankara in order to bring the administration and government closer to central Anatolia. This decision reflected Ataturk's efforts to free the country from the cultural and political legacy of the Ottoman Empire and to form a new national identity based on the principle of republican unity.

In the first decades of the republic, Turkey focused on modernizing its economy and infrastructure, with a focus on industrialization, building educational institutions, and promoting social equality. Ataturk's reforms had a profound impact on all aspects of public life, from clothing to architecture, from language to education.

After Ataturk's death in 1938, his successors continued his modernization agenda while the country faced geopolitical challenges such as World War II and the Cold War. Turkey joined NATO in 1952 and sought a close partnership with the West, while maintaining its relations with neighboring countries in the Middle East and the Caucasus.

Turkey experienced political instability and military coups in the 1960s and 1970s, which affected the country's democratic development. In the 1980s, however, the country began a phase of economic liberalization and opened up more to international trade and investment.

In the 21st century, Turkey has taken on a significant role as a regional player in the Middle East and the geopolitical arena. It has established itself as a dynamic economic power based on agriculture, industry, and tourism, with Istanbul acting as a center for trade, culture, and finance.

Turkey today faces challenges and opportunities in an increasingly globalized world. The political developments, the economic reforms and the social changes reflect the changes that the country has undergone since its founding as a modern republic. The history of the Republic of Turkey is marked by a continuous search for national identity, development and prosperity for its citizens.

Economy and Trade in Turkey

Turkey's economy is one of the largest and most dynamic in the Middle East and Southeastern Europe region. The country has a diverse economic structure based on agriculture, industry, and services. Turkey is known for its fertile soils, which allow for a variety of agricultural products such as grains, cotton, olives, citrus fruits, and vegetables. Agricultural products represent a significant part of the country's exports and contribute to food security and employment in rural areas.

Turkey's industrial sector has made significant progress in recent decades and includes areas such as automotive manufacturing, textile production, electronics, mechanical engineering, chemistry, and construction. Turkey is also a major producer and exporter of steel and has developed a growing presence in the high-tech industry, especially in areas such as information technology and telecommunications.

The service sector is the largest economic sector in Turkey and includes sectors such as tourism, financial services, retail, and hospitality. Istanbul plays a key role as a commercial and financial center for Turkey, serving as a bridge between East and West for international business.

Turkey has a strong export orientation and exports a wide variety of goods and services to countries around the world. The main export products include textiles and apparel, automotive parts, electronics, machinery, and chemical products. Turkey has benefited from its geographical location, which makes it an important trade hub between Europe, the Middle East, Central Asia and Africa.

Over the years, Turkey has carried out significant reforms to liberalize its economy and improve investment conditions. The country has pursued stable macroeconomic policies and implemented a number of structural reforms to support growth and strengthen resilience to external shocks.

Nevertheless, Turkey faces economic challenges, including high unemployment, inequality and a growing trade deficit. Inflation is another ongoing problem that affects the purchasing power of the population and affects the economic stability of the country.

Turkey continues to strive for greater integration into the global economy and is looking for new ways to diversify its trade relations and increase its competitiveness. The challenges of the future require sustainable economic development, investment in education and innovation, and improved infrastructure to realize the country's full economic potential.

Turkish society and population

Turkish society is characterized by a rich cultural diversity and a history that dates back to ancient times. With a population of more than 80 million people, Turkey is one of the most populous countries in the Middle East and Southeastern Europe region. The majority of the population are Turks, who are a Turkic-speaking ethnic group and live mainly in the western part of the country. However, there are also significant minorities, including Kurds, who live in the south-east of the country and retain their own cultural identity.

Turkey has a young population, with a majority of people under the age of 30. Urbanization has increased in recent decades, with cities such as Istanbul, Ankara, Izmir, and Bursa being among the most densely populated and economically dynamic areas in the country. These cities function not only as economic centers but also as cultural and social hubs that offer a wide range of lifestyles and cultural activities.

The traditional Turkish family plays an important role in the social fabric of society. Family ties are strong, and multigenerational households are still common. Respect for older family members and the cultivation of family relationships are essential cultural values. The role of women has changed over the years, with women increasingly gaining access to education and job opportunities, while traditional role models continue to influence.

Religious practices and traditions are deeply rooted in Turkish society. Although Turkey is officially a secular republic, Islam plays a significant role in the daily lives of many people, especially in rural areas and smaller towns. Mosques are centers of religious and social life, and religious holidays are celebrated nationwide. At the same time, there is also a growing number of people who identify as secular or non-religious.

Education is another important aspect of Turkish society, with the education system ranging from kindergarten to university. The literacy rate is high compared to other countries in the region, with the government making increased efforts in recent years to improve access to education and increase the quality of education. Universities in major cities attract students from all over Turkey and play a key role in developing the country's intellectual and scientific potential.

Turkish society is facing challenges such as social inequality, unemployment and demographic changes, which are exacerbated by migration, both within the country and internationally. The integration of refugees from Syria and other countries has also led to social and economic challenges, but has also contributed to new cultural and social dynamics within society.

Overall, Turkish society is a fascinating interplay of tradition and modernity, cultural diversity and social changes. The people of Turkey are proud of their history and culture, while striving to take on the challenges of modernity and further develop their country's potential as a dynamic and diverse nation.

Turkish Culture: Traditions and Customs

Turkish culture is rich in traditions and customs that are deeply rooted in the country's history. These traditions are reflected in various aspects of daily life, from festivals and celebrations to social norms and family structures.

One of the outstanding features of Turkish culture is hospitality. Hosts are known for giving their guests a warm welcome and offering them an abundance of food and drinks. This hospitality is an important part of social interaction and is evident on various occasions such as weddings, birthday parties or religious festivals.

Traditional Turkish cuisine is famous for its variety and refined flavors. Dishes such as kebab, meze (appetizers), baklava and çay (Turkish tea) are popular and reflect the country's regional differences. Eating is more than just a food intake; it is a social event that brings family and friends together.

Religious festivals play a significant role in the Turkish calendar, with the Islamic fasting month of Ramadan being one of the most important religious events. During Ramadan, Muslims fast during the day and break the fast at sunset with iftar, a festive meal often shared with family and friends.

Turkish music and dance traditions have a long history, ranging from classical Ottoman music to modern pop and folklore styles. Traditional musical instruments such as the saz (a long-necked lute) and the kemençe (a three-stringed violin) are part of the country's cultural heritage and are often played on festive occasions.

Handicrafts such as carpet weaving, ceramics making and blacksmithing are also widespread in Turkey and have a long tradition. Techniques that are thousands of years old are still passed on today in craft workshops and workshops in different regions of the country.

Turkish weddings are often opulent and colorful, with festive ceremonies, music, and traditional dances such as the Halay, a circle dance danced by men and women together. Weddings are an opportunity for family and friends to come together and celebrate the union of two families.

Language and literature play a central role in Turkish culture. The Turkish language belongs to the group of Turkic languages and has developed over centuries. Turkish literature includes epic poems such as the "Dede Korkut" and modern works by writers such as Orhan Pamuk, who won the Nobel Prize for Literature.

Sport is also an important part of Turkish culture, with football being the most popular sport. Turkey has a passionate football fan base that supports its national and international teams. Other popular sports include basketball, volleyball, and wrestling.

Overall, Turkish culture is a fascinating mosaic of traditions that reflect the country's history and diversity. These traditions have endured over the centuries and shape the daily life and identity of the people of Turkey.

Turkey's Modern Art Scene

Turkey's modern art scene has developed into a dynamic and diverse movement in recent decades, attracting both national and international attention. Istanbul, as a cultural and economic hub, plays a central role in the country's art scene, followed by other cities such as Ankara and Izmir, which are also home to significant art communities.

Turkish modern art reflects the country's complex history and cultural diversity. Artists experiment with a variety of media and forms of expression, from painting and sculpture to installations, video and performance art. Many modern Turkish artists are internationally known and have participated in prestigious exhibitions and biennials worldwide.

Art education in Turkey is well established, with a variety of art colleges and universities offering programs in fine arts, design, architecture, and other creative disciplines. These institutions play a key role in nurturing young talent and developing innovative approaches to the arts.

The Turkish art scene is characterized by a mixture of traditional influences and contemporary currents. Many artists draw on historical motifs, cultural symbols and local traditions to explore contemporary themes and issues. This results in a unique synthesis of past and present in contemporary Turkish art.

Istanbul is home to a variety of galleries, museums, and art centers that promote and showcase modern Turkish art. The Istanbul Biennial, an international art exhibition held every two years, has established itself as a major forum for contemporary art, attracting art lovers from all over the world.

Turkish artists are known for their critical attitude towards social and political issues. Many artworks reflect Turkey's complex social and cultural challenges, as well as the global developments that shape the modern world. This artistic response to current events and social trends contributes to the diversity and resilience of the Turkish art scene.

The international relations of the Turkish art scene are also significant. Many Turkish artists work globally and participate in international residency programs to gain new perspectives and expand their creative network. These international connections contribute to the global recognition and appreciation of Turkish art.

Overall, Turkey's modern art scene is a vibrant and dynamic field that is continuously evolving and producing new talents. Through its diversity, innovation and critical reflection, Turkish art makes a significant contribution to the cultural life of the country and beyond.

The architecture of mosques in Turkey

The architecture of mosques in Turkey is a fascinating testimony to the religious, cultural and architectural development of the country over centuries. Mosques are not only places of prayer, but also symbols of Muslim identity and artistic expression.

The oldest mosques in Turkey date back to the time of the Ottoman Empire and reflect the architectural styles of that era. Early Ottoman mosques are characterized by their simple construction, often with a central dome and minaret. This structural simplicity was later developed through intricate designs and embellishments inspired by Persian and Arabic influences.

A prominent feature of Ottoman mosque architecture is the use of domes, often topped by hemispherical roofs. These domes symbolize cosmic order and are often surrounded by smaller half-domes and columns that support the building and create a harmonious balance.

The main mosque, or Sultanahmet Mosque, in Istanbul is an outstanding example of classical Ottoman architecture. Built in the 17th century under Sultan Ahmed I, it is known for its six slender minarets and magnificent dome structure. The interiors are adorned with ornate Iznik tiles and marble embellishments that reflect the craftsmanship of the time.

Another important development in Turkish mosque architecture was the introduction of columnar basilicas, which were influenced by Byzantium. This construction method was adopted in Ottoman mosques and led to larger and more spacious buildings that could accommodate a larger number of worshippers.

Over time, Ottoman architecture continued to evolve and incorporate new technological and aesthetic innovations. The Suleymaniye Mosque, also in Istanbul, is a masterpiece of 16th-century Ottoman architecture designed by Sinan, one of the most important architects in Ottoman history. The mosque impresses with its monumental dome and its symmetrical arrangement of minarets and outbuildings.

Modern Turkish mosque architecture is characterized by a synthesis of traditional elements and contemporary design. Many new mosques in Turkey are remarkable examples of contemporary architecture that combines functionality with aesthetic sophistication. They use modern building materials and techniques, while respecting the traditional values and principles of mosque architecture.

Overall, mosques in Turkey are not only architectural masterpieces, but also symbols of the country's cultural and religious identity. They are places of spiritual reflection and social cohesion that play a central role in the lives of the people of Turkey.

The Cuisine of Turkey: A Culinary Journey

Turkey's cuisine is known for its diversity and rich flavor, which is the result of a rich culinary history that dates back to ancient times. Turkish cuisine combines influences from the Middle East, Central Asia, the Mediterranean, and the Balkans to create a unique culinary tradition that is prized for its variety of flavors and sophistication.

One of the central components of Turkish cuisine is olive oil, which is used in many dishes, from salads to appetizers and main courses. Fresh herbs such as parsley, dill, mint and coriander also play an important role and give the dishes their characteristic taste.

The traditional Turkish breakfast is rich and varied, often consisting of olives, cheese, tomatoes, cucumbers, eggs, bread and jam. A popular breakfast dish is the "simit", a ring of baked dough with sesame seeds, which is often enjoyed with tea, which plays a big role in everyday life in Turkey.

Meat dishes are also an essential part of Turkish cuisine, especially lamb, beef, and poultry. Kebabs are known worldwide and include different variants, such as the Adana Kebab or the

Döner Kebab, which is prepared using a special vertical grilling technique and is often served with flatbread and yoghurt sauce.

One of the signature desserts of Turkish cuisine is baklava, a puff pastry with nuts and syrup that is enjoyed both as a dessert and on special occasions. Turkish honey, also known as "muhallebi," is another popular dessert that is often sprinkled with cinnamon and has a creamy consistency.

Turkish cuisine is also known for its variety of meze, small appetizers and appetizers that are often served at the beginning of a meal. Popular meze include hummus, babaganoush (smoked eggplant dip), tzatziki, and various salads seasoned with olive oil and lemon juice.

A special feature of Turkish cuisine is the regional differences, which are due to the geographical diversity of the country. The coastal regions offer an abundance of seafood and fish dishes, while the interior is known for its meat dishes and the use of legumes such as lentils and beans.

Turkish specialties such as "manti" (stuffed dumplings), "köfte" (Turkish meatballs) and "dolma" (stuffed vegetables such as vine leaves or peppers) are popular dishes that reflect the craftsmanship and culinary sophistication of Turkish cuisine.

In recent years, Turkish cuisine has also gained international prominence, with Turkish restaurants spreading around the world and impressing people with their variety and taste. Turkish cuisine is not only a source of enjoyment, but also a cultural heritage that reflects the country's identity and history.

Turkey's Wine and Beverage Culture

Turkey's wine and beverage culture is diverse, reflecting the country's rich history and geographical diversity. Winegrowing has a long tradition in Turkey that dates back to ancient times. Especially the region of Thrace in the northwest and Anatolia in the west and south of the country are known for their wine production.

One of the most famous Turkish wines is raki, a traditional drink often referred to as "Turkish anise liquor". Raki is usually diluted with water and served with meze (appetizers). It is an important part of Turkish food culture and is often enjoyed on social occasions and celebrations.

In addition to raki, tea is a central element in Turkish beverage culture. Turkish tea is served strong and hot and is an integral part of the daily life of people in Turkey. Teahouses, known as "Çay Bahçesi" or "Çay Evi", are popular meeting places where people come together to drink tea and chat.

Turkish coffee culture is also remarkable. The Turkish coffee, known as "Türk Kahvesi", is served strong and unsweetened in small cups and is known for its rich flavor and aromatic intensity.

Coffee houses are traditional places for socializing and discussing current events.

In recent years, the craft beer scene in Turkey has developed dynamically, especially in larger cities such as Istanbul and Ankara. Microbreweries produce a variety of craft beers that use local ingredients and traditional brewing techniques, while keeping in mind international trends in beer culture.

Turkish sodas and fruit juices are also popular, especially on hot summer days. Ayran, a yogurt drink with salt, is a refreshing and healthy drink that is often served with traditional dishes such as kebabs.

Turkey's religious and cultural diversity is also reflected in its beverage culture. Alcoholic beverages such as raki are enjoyed by many Turks, while others, especially in more conservative regions, reject alcohol and prefer traditional drinks instead.

Overall, Turkey's wine and beverage culture is a multifaceted mosaic of traditional and modern elements that enriches the social interaction and daily life of the people in the country. The variety of drinks reflects the diversity of Turkish society and its openness to new influences and innovations.

Turkish Music: Tradition and Modernity

Turkish music is a fascinating interplay of tradition and modernity that reflects the cultural diversity and historical influences of the country. Over the centuries, a rich musical tradition has developed, integrating both local and international elements, giving rise to a variety of genres and styles.

Traditional Turkish music has its roots in ancient times and has been influenced by various cultural currents throughout history. Traditional musical instruments include the saz, a long-necked lute, the bağlama, a short-necked lute, and the kemençe, a three-stringed violin. These instruments are often accompanied by musicians who interpret folk songs or epic poems known as "Türkü".

An important feature of Turkish music is the "makam" system, which is a kind of melodic scale and plays a central role in the structure and improvisation of traditional pieces of music. Each "makam" has a unique emotional and aesthetic quality, which is defined by the choice of pitches and rhythmic patterns.

Ottoman court music, known as "Classical Turkish Music", developed from a mixture of

Persian, Arabic and Byzantine influences and was cultivated for centuries at the court of the sultans. This musical tradition includes instrumental works as well as vocal compositions, often performed by choirs or solo singers.

With modernization and Western influence in the 20th century, the Turkish music landscape began to diversify. New genres such as Turkish pop, rock, hip-hop, and electronic music gained popularity, incorporating Western harmonies and instruments into the traditional forms.

Turkish pop music stars such as Tarkan and Sezen Aksu gained international fame and contributed to the spread of Turkish music beyond the country's borders. Their songs often combine traditional elements with modern production techniques, reflecting contemporary themes and styles.

The Turkish music industry is now one of the most dynamic in the region, producing a variety of music videos, albums, and live concerts that appeal to a wide audience. Istanbul is the center of this cultural development, with numerous music studios, concert halls and festivals taking place throughout the year.

Turkish folk music, such the zeybek (a traditional dance from the Aegean region) and the horon (a dance from the Black Sea region), continue to be living expressions of local identity and community. These dances are often accompanied by traditional music that preserves the heritage and history of the regions from which they originate.

Overall, Turkey's musical landscape is a dynamic synthesis of past and present, reflecting the country's cultural identity while exploring new creative avenues. This diversity and innovation make Turkish music a fascinating window into the soul and life of the people of Turkey.

Turkey's Literary Scene

Turkey's literary scene is rich in diversity and history, dating back to the country's early civilizational beginnings. Turkish literature has a long tradition of poetry, narrative and dramatic performance, which has been shaped by different historical periods. One of the earliest forms of Turkish literature was the oral tradition of epic poems and legends handed down by the early Turkic tribes in Central Asia. With the introduction of Islam in the 11th century, Turkish literature continued to develop and was strongly influenced by Arabic and Persian influences. Classical works such as the "Divan" poetry by poets such as Rumi and Yunus Emre remain significant examples of the spiritual and poetic expressiveness of Turkish literature to this day.

During the Ottoman era, Turkish literature flourished, especially with the introduction of printing in the 19th century, which facilitated the dissemination of books and literary works. Ottoman poets and writers such as Fuzuli, Nedim, and Şeyh Galip shaped this era with their works in various literary genres, including poetry, epic, and prose. Ottoman literature was also heavily influenced by mystical and philosophical themes that reflected the complex worldview and values of the empire.

In the 20th century, Turkish literature experienced a renaissance with the founding of modern Turkey under Mustafa Kemal Atatürk. Turkish writers such as Yaşar Kemal, Orhan Pamuk and Elif Şafak gained international recognition for their works that explore both traditional and modern themes and styles. Pamuk, who won the Nobel Prize for Literature in 2006, is known for his introspective novels, which often explore historical and social issues of Turkey.

Today, the Turkish literary scene is diverse and dynamic, with a large number of writers, poets and intellectuals reflecting the country's social and political challenges through their works. Modern Turkish literature encompasses a wide range of genres and themes, from feminist literature to experimental prose and dystopian narratives. Literary festivals such as the Istanbul International Literature Festival attract writers and literature lovers from all over the world every year, providing a platform for sharing and discussing the world of literature.

Turkish literature remains a central part of the country's cultural identity and a source of inspiration and reflection for generations of readers and writers. Through its diversity, depth and artistic sophistication, Turkish literature continues to contribute to the intellectual and cultural landscape of the world.

The education system of Turkey

Turkey's education system has evolved throughout history to meet the growing demands and challenges of society. The foundation of Turkey's modern education system was laid after the founding of the Republic of Turkey in 1923, when Mustafa Kemal Ataturk introduced educational reforms aimed at promoting literacy and modernizing the country. One of the most significant reforms was the introduction of compulsory education for children aged 6 to 14, which continues to this day.

Turkey's education system includes both public and private schools at various levels of education, including kindergarten, primary, secondary school, and university. Access to education is universally accessible and free until the end of high school. However, the quality of educational institutions varies greatly between urban and rural areas, as well as between public and private schools.

Turkey's higher education system has also evolved significantly, including a variety of universities and polytechnics that offer a wide range of degree programs in fields such as engineering, medicine, humanities, business, and science. The number of universities has risen sharply in recent decades, with both state and private institutions playing an important role.

Turkey has made significant efforts in recent years to improve the quality and relevance of its education systems. Reforms often focus on modernising curricula, promoting foreign language skills and integrating information technology into the classroom. Despite these efforts, educational institutions often face challenges such as overcrowded classrooms, limited resources, and regional disparities.

The Turkish government has a strong focus on education and research to promote national development and strengthen economic competitiveness. Programs to promote science and technology and to support talented students and researchers are actively promoted. Turkish universities are increasingly involved in international research collaborations and are striving to achieve a higher ranking in global rankings.

However, Turkey's education system also faces challenges such as integrating refugee children, ensuring gender equality in education, and adapting to changing global education trends. Nevertheless, education remains a priority for Turkey, as it is seen as key to personal and social development, as well as to promote innovation and progress.

Istanbul: The History of a World Metropolis

Istanbul, the former capital of the Byzantine and Ottoman Empires, is a fascinating metropolis whose history spans several millennia. Originally founded as a Byzantium, the city was renamed Constantinople by Emperor Constantine the Great in honor of his own name in 330 AD and became the center of the Eastern Roman Empire. As the capital of the Byzantine Empire, Constantinople flourished as a center of trade, culture, and science in the Middle Ages. The magnificent Hagia Sophia, originally built as a Byzantine cathedral and later used as a mosque and now as a museum, stands as a symbol of this era.

In 1453, Sultan Mehmed II, also known as Mehmed the Conqueror, conquered Constantinople after a long siege and made it the capital of the Ottoman Empire. Under Ottoman rule, Istanbul experienced another cultural heyday and became an important hub for trade, religion and culture between Europe and Asia. The magnificent architecture, including the Blue Mosque and Topkapı Palace, testifies to the splendor and wealth of this era.

Istanbul's strategic location on the Bosphorus made the city a valuable destination for conquerors from all over the world. Ottoman architecture and culture mixed with European and Oriental influences, resulting in a unique cultural synthesis that is still visible today. The city served as a bridge between East and West, a place where different cultures, religions and traditions met and mixed.

In the early 20th century, Istanbul became the center of the modern Turkish Republic under the leadership of Mustafa Kemal Ataturk. The capital was later moved to Ankara, but Istanbul remained the cultural and economic heart of Turkey. The city experienced rapid urban development and grew into one of the most populous metropolises in the world, with a dynamic economy, a vibrant art scene and a rich cultural heritage.

Today, Istanbul is a modern world metropolis that combines old and new elements in a unique mix. The city's historic districts such as Sultanahmet and the Galata region offer a glimpse into the city's rich history, while modern districts such as Beyoğlu and Levent are the economic and cultural center. The Bosphorus, which divides the city into the European and Asian parts, remains a lively waterway that promotes trade and cultural interaction.

Istanbul remains a fascinating melting pot of cultures, a place where history and modernity meet, creating a dynamic and vibrant atmosphere. The city continues to attract visitors from all over the world, attracted by its history, architecture, food, and hospitality, and remains an indispensable symbol of Turkey's cultural diversity and richness.

Istanbul Today: Modernity and Tradition in Transition

Istanbul, the vibrant metropolis on the Bosporus, is today a fascinating synthesis of modernity and tradition that is constantly changing. As Turkey's largest city and a historical link between Europe and Asia, Istanbul plays a central role in the region's geopolitical, cultural and economic landscape. Home to over 15 million people, the city is a melting pot of different ethnicities, religions, and lifestyles that blend harmoniously and influence each other.

Modern skyscrapers in neighborhoods such as Levent and Maslak stand in stark contrast to the historic buildings of the Old City, such as the Hagia Sophia and the Blue Mosque. This architectural diversity reflects how Istanbul cleverly blends the old and new elements while retaining its character and identity. The expansion of the public transport system, including the metro and modern tram lines, has helped to improve mobility in the city and cope with the growing traffic.

Istanbul's economic importance is evident in its role as Turkey's leading financial center, with a thriving economy that relies on industries such as trade, tourism, finance, and technology. The city is home to numerous international companies and is an important hub for global trade routes, especially through the Bosphorus, which serves as a strategic waterway for transporting goods between Europe and Asia.

Culturally, Istanbul is a treasure trove of museums, art galleries, theaters, and concert halls that reflect the city's rich heritage. Istanbul Modern, Pera Museum, and Topkapı Palace are just a few of the places that attract visitors who want to explore the city's art, history, and culture. In addition, Istanbul is known for its vibrant music scene, from traditional Turkish music to modern interpretations in clubs and concert halls.

Istanbul's culinary richness reflects the diversity of its inhabitants, offering a wealth of flavors from Turkish cuisine as well as international influences. Street markets, such as the Grand Bazaar and Egyptian Bazaar, offer local specialties, spices, handicrafts, and more that are at the heart of Turkish culture.

Politically, Istanbul is a central arena for national and international affairs, as it serves as the seat of the Turkish government and the site of important international conferences and summits. The city plays a key role in promoting peace and stability in the region and is at the heart of efforts to achieve sustainable development and social justice.

Istanbul is also a city of contrasts and challenges. Despite its rapid economic growth, issues such as urban pollution, social inequality, and the preservation of historical heritage are at the center of public discussions and policy decisions. Nevertheless, Istanbul remains a vibrant, dynamic city that fascinates with its diversity and wealth of culture, history and innovation, attracting visitors from all over the world.

Ankara: Capital of Turkey

Ankara, the capital of Turkey, is a city rich in history, political significance and cultural diversity. Originally founded as Ancyra in the ancient Roman province of Galatia, Ankara has played a strategic role as a crossroads between East and West since ancient times. The city was later controlled by the Byzantines and then by the Seljuks before falling under Ottoman rule in the 13th century. Under Ottoman rule, Ankara was a provincial city in the shadow of Istanbul for a long time, but it gained importance after the fall of the Ottoman Empire.

With the founding of modern Turkey in 1923 by Mustafa Kemal Ataturk, Ankara was declared the capital to mark a symbolic and practical break with the Ottoman past and to modernize the country. Ataturk initiated comprehensive reforms, including the introduction of a modern legal system and the secularization of the state, which consolidated Ankara as a political center.

Today, Ankara is not only the political, but also the economic and cultural centre of Turkey. The city is home to important government institutions, including the presidential palace and the Turkish parliament, as well as numerous embassies and international organizations. Ankara is also an important educational hub with a number of renowned universities and research institutions.

Ankara's modern infrastructure includes an extensive network of roads, bridges and public transport, facilitating mobility within the city and beyond its borders. The city is known for its leafy parks and wide boulevards that contrast with the narrow streets and historic buildings of the Old Town.

Culturally, Ankara offers an abundance of museums, theaters, galleries, and cultural centers that reflect the rich history and diversity of Turkish culture. The Museum of Anatolian Civilizations and the Ataturk Mausoleum (Anıtkabir) are significant historical sites that attract visitors and offer insights into the history and development of the region.

Ankara is also known for its diverse culinary scene, which includes traditional Turkish cuisine as well as international influences. Markets and restaurants offer a wide range of cuisines, from local specialties to international delicacies.

Politically, Ankara remains a centre of decision-making and political dialogue not only at the national level, but also at the international level. The city plays a key role in promoting diplomacy and cooperation between different countries and cultures, while at the same time strengthening its own identity as the capital of Turkey.

Izmir: The pearl of the Aegean Sea

Izmir, known as the Pearl of the Aegean Sea, is one of the most important cities on Turkey's west coast and a significant economic, cultural and historical center. The city has a long and rich history that dates back to ancient times, when it was known by various names such as Smyrna. Its favorable location on the Aegean Sea and its protected harbor contributed to the development of Izmir as an important trading and seaport, facilitating the exchange of goods and cultures between the Mediterranean, the Middle East, and Europe.

Izmir experienced a heyday during Greek and Roman rule, when it became a major trading center and a thriving city. Important archaeological sites such as Ephesus, one of the largest and best-preserved ancient cities in the world, bear witness to this historical significance and attract visitors from all over the world.

Over the centuries, Izmir has been shaped by various civilizations, including the Ottomans, who conquered the city in the 15th century, making it an important administrative center and trading port. Under Ottoman rule, Izmir experienced a cultural heyday and developed into a melting pot of different cultural and religious influences that are still visible today.

During the 19th and early 20th centuries, Izmir became a major trading center for the export of agricultural products such as olive oil, wine, and cotton, contributing to the economic prosperity of the region. However, the city also experienced political unrest and was severely damaged during the Greco-Turkish War of 1919-1922.

After the founding of modern Turkey under Mustafa Kemal Ataturk in 1923, Izmir experienced a period of recovery and modernization. The city became an important commercial and industrial center and played a key role in promoting Western values and modernizing the country.

Today, Izmir is a modern metropolis with a population of over 4 million people and a dynamic economy based on industries such as shipbuilding, trade, tourism, textiles, and technology. The city is known for its hospitable people, vibrant cultural scene, and picturesque beaches along the Aegean Sea.

Culturally, Izmir offers a variety of museums, galleries, theaters, and music events that reflect the region's rich heritage. Izmir's Old Town, known as Konak, is a popular destination for visitors who want to explore the traditional Turkish architecture, narrow streets, and historic buildings.

The culinary scene in Izmir is equally diverse and reflects the rich Aegean cuisine, which is characterized by fresh seafood, olive oil, herbs and local products. Markets like Kemeraltı Bazaar offer a wealth of flavors and flavors that delight visitors.

Izmir remains a city in transition, celebrating its rich history and cultural diversity as it evolves and adapts to the challenges and opportunities of the modern world. As the gateway to the Aegean Sea and a bridge between East and West, Izmir remains an essential destination for travelers who want to experience the beauty, history, and hospitality of Turkey's Aegean.

Antalya and the Turkish Riviera

Antalya and the Turkish Riviera are known for their breathtaking beauty, rich history, and a variety of tourist attractions. Located on the southern coast of Turkey at the eastern end of the Mediterranean coast, the Antalya region is one of the country's most popular holiday destinations. The history of Antalya dates back to ancient times, when the city was known as Attaleia, named after King Attalos II of Pergamon.

Antalya's Old Town, called Kaleiçi, is a maze of narrow streets, historic buildings, and remnants from Byzantine, Roman, and Ottoman periods. The Yivli Minaret, a 13th-century landmark of the city, stands as a testament to Ottoman architecture and is an important symbol of Antalya's history and culture.

The Turkish Riviera stretches along the coast of Antalya and includes picturesque towns and villages such as Side, Alanya, Kemer and Kas. These places offer not only magnificent beaches with crystal clear waters, but also an abundance of ancient sites that attract visitors from all over the world. Side, for example, was once an important port city of ancient Pamphylia and is now known for its well-preserved ancient theater and the Temple of Apollo right by the sea.

Alanya, known for its impressive fortress on a hill above the city, offers spectacular views of the Mediterranean Sea and is a popular destination for visitors who want to enjoy history and nature in equal measure. The red towers of Alanya Fortress, built in the 13th century during the Seljuk period, dominate the coastline and offer a glimpse of the military architecture of the time.

Kemer, a picturesque resort town south of Antalya, beckons with its luxurious resorts, marinas and the Taurus Mountains in the background. The surrounding nature offers hiking trails through pine forests and along the coast that delight outdoor enthusiasts and nature lovers alike.

Kas, a charming fishing village, is known for its laid-back atmosphere, diving opportunities, and the remains of an ancient Lycian city that lies nearby. The colorful marine life off the coast of Kas makes it a popular destination for divers and snorkelers who want to explore the beauty of the Mediterranean.

The Turkish Riviera is also known for its world-class resorts and hotels, which offer a wide range of accommodation and services, from luxury all-inclusive resorts to boutique hotels in historic buildings. These accommodations offer not only comfort and hospitality, but also access to the many sights and activities of the region.

The cuisine of the Turkish Riviera is characterized by fresh seafood, olive oil, herbs and local products, which are offered in the region's numerous restaurants, cafes and street markets. Visitors can enjoy local specialties such as grilled fish, meze (appetizers) and baklava (a traditional Turkish dessert) as they discover the culinary diversity and richness of the region.

Overall, Antalya and the Turkish Riviera is a region of outstanding beauty, historical significance, and a wealth of opportunities for visitors who want to experience Turkey's sun, sea, and rich culture. From ancient ruins to modern resorts, the region offers something for everyone and remains an essential destination for tourists from all over the world.

Cappadocia: Fairytale landscape of Turkey

Cappadocia, the fairytale landscape of Turkey, is a region of unparalleled beauty and historical significance in central Anatolia. Known for its unique geological formation known as "fairy chimneys" or "rock cities," Cappadocia attracts visitors from all over the world every year, drawn by the surreal landscape and rich history.

The characteristic fairy chimneys of Cappadocia are the result of volcanic activity millions of years ago, which has resulted in a landscape of soft tuff stones that have been shaped into bizarre shapes over time by wind and water. Often converted by human hands into 4th-century dwellings and churches, these cone-shaped rocks are a fascinating sight and give a glimpse into the area's early Christian history.

Cappadocia was a significant center of early Christianity during the Byzantine era and became a haven for early Christians fleeing persecution. The rock-hewn churches of Cappadocia, such as the Goreme Open Air Museum, which is a UNESCO World Heritage Site, are adorned with frescoes and religious representations that offer a glimpse into the religious life and culture of the time.

However, the history of Cappadocia goes back much further than early Christianity. The region was once home to various civilizations, including the Hittites, Persians, Romans, and Byzantines, all of whom have left their mark. Numerous ancient ruins, fortresses and troglodyte dwellings bear witness to this rich history and offer visitors the opportunity to immerse themselves in the past.

In addition to its historical significance, Cappadocia is also known for its unique culture and hospitality. Traditional crafts, such as carpet weaving, ceramics and wood carving, are still maintained here and are part of the heritage that has been passed down from generation to generation. Markets and bazaars offer visitors the chance to experience local crafts and pick up souvenirs that reflect the culture of the area.

The landscape of Cappadocia is impressive not only at the top of the earth, but also below the surface. The tuff formations are crisscrossed by underground cities and tunnels that were used by the inhabitants of the region as protection from invaders and the elements. Places like Derinkuyu and Kaymaklı are well-known underground cities that visitors can explore to get a glimpse of the everyday life of the ancient inhabitants.

Today, Cappadocia is not only a popular tourist destination, but also a center for adventure vacationers and nature lovers. Hot air balloon rides over the stunning landscape of Cappadocia offer unforgettable views of the fairy chimneys and picturesque valleys, while hiking and horseback riding tours through the valleys and vineyards of the region offer a unique way to experience nature.

The cuisine of Cappadocia is characterized by local products such as wine, honey, olive oil and fresh herbs, which are offered in the numerous restaurants and local inns of the region. Visitors can sample traditional dishes such as testi kebabı (tonkebab) and mantı (Turkish dumplings) while enjoying the culinary delights of the region.

Overall, Cappadocia is a region of outstanding beauty, history, and culture that attracts visitors from all over the world and offers them an unforgettable journey into one of Turkey's most fascinating landscapes.

The ancient cities of Pamukkale and Ephesus

Pamukkale and Ephesus are among Turkey's most impressive ancient cities, each with its own unique history and architectural splendor. Pamukkale, which translates to "cotton castle", is known worldwide for its spectacular limestone terraces, which were formed by mineral deposits from hot springs over thousands of years. These natural formations, which look like frozen waterfalls, offer not only a picturesque picture, but also a therapeutic spring that has been prized for its healing properties since ancient times.

In ancient times, Pamukkale was known as Hierapolis, an ancient city built on the thermal springs above the terraces. Hierapolis was an important city in the Roman province of Asia and prospered thanks to its strategic location on the trade routes between Asia Minor, Greece and Rome. The ruins of Hierapolis include well-preserved theaters, temples, necropolises, and an extensive Roman bathhouse complex that was used to exploit the thermal springs.

Ephesus, another outstanding ancient city, is located on the west coast of Turkey and was one of the largest and most important cities in the region in ancient times. The history of Ephesus dates back to the Bronze Age Aegean Sea and was known for its Temple of Artemis, one of the Seven Wonders of the Ancient World. During Roman rule, Ephesus flourished as a center of trade, culture, and religion and was an important city of early Christianity.

The ruins of Ephesus, now a UNESCO World Heritage Site, offer a fascinating glimpse into life in an ancient metropolis. The Great Theater of Ephesus, which held up to 25,000 spectators, was a center for political and cultural events, while the Library of Celsus, an impressive Roman-style structure, was considered one of the largest libraries in the ancient world.

The ancient city was also an important religious center and the place where the apostle Paul preached. The remains of the Basilica of St. John and the House of the Virgin Mary near Ephesus are important pilgrimage sites for Christians from all over the world.

Both ancient cities, Pamukkale and Ephesus, not only offer a window into Turkey's past, but are also witnesses to the cultural and architectural achievements of their time. They attract millions of visitors every year who want to experience the beauty and heritage of these extraordinary places that have played a significant role in the history of mankind.

The Black Sea region: culture and nature

The Black Sea region of Turkey is a fascinating mix of rich culture and stunning nature, stretching along the coast from the eastern Black Sea to the western coast. This region is known for its lush green landscapes, favored by the mild, humid climate characterized by its proximity to the sea.

The history of the Black Sea region dates back to ancient times, when it was an important center of Greek colonization. Known for its Byzantine and Ottoman history, the city of Trabzon (Trebizond) was once an important trading center on the Black Sea and is now a popular destination for visitors looking to explore the region's cultural diversity and historical treasures.

In addition to its rich history, the Black Sea region is also known for its unique architecture, which has been shaped by the different civilizations that have lived here over the centuries. Typical of the region are traditional wooden houses decorated with elaborate carvings, a testimony to craftsmanship and local architecture.

The Black Sea region's coastline is lined with quaint fishing villages and small towns known for their hospitality and traditional cuisine. The local cuisine is characterized by fresh seafood, such as grilled fish and various seafood dishes that have been passed down from generation to generation. The region is also known for its varieties of tea, which are grown and harvested in the tea plantations along the hills.

In addition to its cultural significance, the Black Sea region is also a paradise for nature lovers who appreciate the unspoiled beauty and diversity of the landscape. National parks such as Yedigöller National Park offer hiking trails through dense forests and to crystal-clear lakes fed by the mountains. These areas are home to a variety of plant and animal species, including rare bird species, making the region a hotspot for birdwatchers.

Another characteristic feature of the Black Sea region is the numerous waterfalls that pour down from the mountains into the valley, offering spectacular views. A popular destination for nature lovers, Lake Uzungöl is surrounded by dense forests and provides an idyllic backdrop for recreation and recreation in nature.

Overall, the Black Sea region of Turkey is a region of unparalleled beauty and diversity, captivating visitors with its rich history, cultural heritage, and breathtaking landscapes. Whether exploring the historic cities, sampling traditional dishes or exploring nature, the Black Sea region offers something for everyone and remains an essential destination for explorers and epicureans alike.

The Lycian coast and its ancient sites

The Lycian coast of Turkey stretches along the southwestern coast of the country and is known for its impressive landscape of turquoise blue waters, jagged rocks and picturesque bays. This region, named after the ancient Lycian people, is home to a variety of ancient sites that bear witness to a rich history and culture.

One of the outstanding ancient sites along the Lycian coast is Xanthos, one of the most important cities of the ancient Lycian civilization. Xanthos was once the capital of the Lycian League and is known for its monumental tombs and well-preserved theater, which offers impressive views of the surrounding valley. The city played an important role in the military and political conflicts of the region during ancient times.

Another significant highlight along the Lycian coast is Patara, an ancient city and port city known for its long sandy beach and was one of the largest cities in the Lycian League. Patara was not only an important trading center, but also the birthplace of Saint Nicholas, who is revered as the forerunner of modern Santa Claus. The remains of Patara include a well-preserved theater, thermal baths, and Roman roads that take visitors back to the time of Roman rule.

Another notable ancient site along the Lycian coast is the city of Myra, famous for its well-preserved rock tombs and ancient theater. Myra was a significant center of early Christianity and is known as the place where Saint Nicholas, also known as Santa Claus, served as a bishop. The remains of the Church of St. Nicholas are an important place of pilgrimage for Christians from all over the world.

The Lycian coast offers not only historical treasures, but also a spectacular natural environment that is ideal for sailing, diving and hiking. The coast is lined with countless small islands and bays that provide perfect anchorages for sailboats and give visitors the opportunity to explore secluded beaches and hidden caves.

The region is also known for its unique architecture, including the famous Lycian rock tombs carved into the steep slopes of the mountains, which contain elaborate reliefs and inscriptions that offer insight into the lives and traditions of the Lycian people. These tombs are an outstanding example of the craftsmanship and construction of antiquity and bear witness to the cultural heyday of this region.

Overall, Turkey's Lycian coast is a fascinating destination that enchants visitors with its mix of history, culture, and nature. The ancient sites along the coast offer a fascinating glimpse into the region's past, while the spectacular scenery and warm hospitality of the locals make the Lycian coast an unforgettable destination.

Turkey's Wildlife: From Steppes to Forests

Turkey's wildlife is as diverse as its landscapes, ranging from the arid steppes of Central Anatolia to the dense forests of the Black Sea region. Turkey's geographical location between Europe and Asia, and between the Mediterranean Sea and the Black Sea, creates a rich ecosystem that is home to a wide range of animal species.

In the steppes and semi-deserts of central Anatolia, animals such as the goiter vulture and the golden eagle are often found. These majestic birds of prey use the wide open landscapes to hunt and are a symbol of the region's wilderness. Other typical inhabitants of the steppes are the wild sheep and the steppe gazelle, which have adapted to the dry climate and sparse vegetation.

Along the coasts of the Mediterranean and Aegean Seas, various species of sea turtles are native to the beaches and are protected to maintain their populations. These species include the loggerhead turtle and the green sea turtle, which return to the coasts of Turkey every year to lay their eggs.

The forests of the Black Sea region provide habitat for a variety of mammals, including the brown bear, the Eurasian lynx and the red deer.

These forests are also home to numerous species of birds, including the black stork and the lesser spotted eagle, which appreciate the region's dense forests and rich food sources.

In the mountainous areas of Turkey, such as the Taurus and Pontic Mountains, wild goat species such as the Caucasian ibex and the Anatolian mouflon can be found. These animals are adapted to the harsh climate and steep rock formations and use their dexterity to survive in the challenging mountain landscapes.

Turkey is also home to a variety of predators, including the wolf, golden jackal, and raccoon dog. These animals play an important role in the ecosystem by regulating the balance of animal populations and helping to maintain the health of natural habitats.

In summary, Turkey's wildlife is characterized by its diversity of habitats and climatic conditions. From the vast steppes to the dense forests, Turkey is home to an impressive variety of animal species that are of great importance to both nature lovers and biodiversity conservation.

Environmental Protection and Natural Treasures of Turkey

Environmental protection and the preservation of natural resources play an increasingly important role in Turkey, given the country's diverse ecosystems and rich biodiversity. Turkey spans different climates and geographical regions, from the arid steppes of Central Anatolia to the humid forests of the Black Sea region and the Mediterranean coastal strips. Each of these regions offers a unique variety of plant and animal species, which are often endemic and are unique to Turkey.

A significant focus in Turkey's environmental protection is on the preservation of its natural landscapes and the promotion of sustainable practices in land use. This includes measures to reforest and protect endangered species, including the establishment of national parks and nature reserves. These protected areas serve not only to preserve biodiversity, but also to preserve ecosystem services such as water regulation and soil conservation.

Turkey is rich in natural resources, including a variety of mineral deposits and arable land. The sustainable use of these resources is crucial to prevent pollution and ensure the long-term availability of these resources. The government is increasingly advocating green technologies and practices in industry and agriculture to reduce the country's environmental footprint. Another important issue in Turkey's environmental protection is the protection of marine and coastal ecosystems. Turkey's coastline stretches for several thousand kilometers along the Mediterranean, Aegean, and Black Seas, which serve as important habitats for sea turtles, dolphins, and a variety of fish and coral species. Measures to protect these ecosystems include the creation of marine protected areas, monitoring water quality and regulating fisheries to ensure the sustainable use of marine resources.

Turkey is also actively involved in international environmental protection agreements and cooperates with other countries to address global environmental issues such as climate change and the protection of endangered species. The protection of natural habitats and the promotion of sustainable tourism are essential components of the national environmental strategy, which aims to preserve the beauty and diversity of Turkish nature for generations to come.

Overall, environmental protection and the preservation of Turkey's natural resources is a dynamic and multidimensional issue that encompasses environmental, economic and social aspects. Through targeted measures and awareness among the population, Turkey can continue to play a pioneering role in the sustainable management of its natural resources and ecosystems.

Turkey's Climate: From the Coast to the Highlands

Turkey's climate is extremely diverse and is strongly influenced by its geographical location and different topographies. In general, Turkey can be divided into different climatic regions, ranging from Mediterranean on the coast to continental inland.

On the coast of the Aegean Sea and the Mediterranean Sea, a Mediterranean climate prevails. Summers are hot and dry, while winters are mild and humid. Temperatures in summer can often rise above 30 degrees Celsius, while the winter months are mild and only occasionally result in rainfall. The coastal regions are also known for their pleasant autumn and spring seasons, which offer ideal conditions for tourism.

The Black Sea region in northern Turkey has a humid and temperate climate. Here, rainfall is abundant throughout the year, especially in winter, when the region is affected by humid air masses from the Black Sea. Summers are usually mild and temperatures remain moderate due to the proximity to the sea.

Central Anatolia has a continental climate characterized by hot summers and cold winters. The summer months are hot and dry, with temperatures often exceeding 30 degrees Celsius. Winters, on the other hand, are cold and can reach temperatures below freezing. The seasons are distinct here, with warm spring and fall times ideal for outdoor activities.

The eastern regions of Turkey, especially the areas along the border with Armenia and Iran, have a high alpine climate. Here, winters are long and severe, with heavy snowfall and temperatures that can drop well below freezing. Summers are short and cool, while spring and autumn are rather mild.

Turkey is also vulnerable to extreme weather events such as heat waves, droughts, and occasional floods, which can be exacerbated by climatic fluctuations and climate change. The Government of Turkey is actively working to adapt to these challenges and take measures to mitigate the effects of climate change.

Overall, Turkey's climate shows remarkable diversity and is an important factor in the different habitats and economic activities in the country. The different climatic conditions contribute to the diversity of flora and fauna and shape the cultural traditions and way of life of the people in different regions of Turkey.

The Languages of Turkey: Turkish and Minority Languages

Turkey is known for its linguistic diversity, which is made up of both the dominant official language, Turkish, and a number of minority languages. Turkish is the official and most widely spoken language of the country, spoken by the vast majority of the population. It belongs to the Turkic-speaking group and is closely related to other Central Asian languages such as Azerbaijani and Turkmen. Turkish uses the Latin alphabet, which was introduced in 1928 as part of the Kemalist reforms to promote modernization and literacy in the country.

In addition to Turkish, there are a variety of minority languages spoken by ethnic and religious minorities in Turkey. The most important minority languages include Kurdish, Arabic, Armenian, Greek and Aramaic. These languages are often closely linked to Turkey's history and cultural diversity, reflecting the different ethnic groups that have lived in the region for centuries.

Kurdish is the largest minority language in Turkey and is spoken by the Kurdish population in the southeast of the country. There are several dialects of Kurdish, including Kurmanci, Zazaki, and Sorani, which are spoken in different regions.

In recent years, the Turkish government has taken steps to facilitate the use and promotion of the Kurdish language, although historically there have been political tensions over the recognition and use of Kurdish.

Arabic is mainly spoken by the Arab population in Turkey, especially in cities such as Hatay and Şanlıurfa, which have a significant Arab population. Arabic has a historical and cultural impact on Turkey, especially through its connection to Islam and long-standing trade and cultural ties with Arabic-speaking countries.

Armenian and Greek are other significant minority languages spoken mainly in Istanbul and on the Aegean coast, where historically a large Armenian and Greek population lived. These languages contribute to Turkey's cultural diversity and heritage, and are often closely linked to the history of Ottoman rule and relations with neighboring countries.

Aramaic is spoken by the Aramaic community in Turkey, an ethnic and religious minority that historically lived in the Mesopotamia region. Today, there are still some communities in Turkey that speak Aramaic, especially in southeastern Anatolia.

Turkey's linguistic diversity not only reflects its multicultural society, but also represents a challenge and an opportunity for national unity and cultural heritage. The Turkish government is increasingly committed to the protection and promotion of minority languages in order to preserve the country's linguistic diversity while promoting national integration.

Turkish customs and festivals throughout the year

Turkish culture is rich in traditional customs and festivals that are celebrated throughout the year and offer a deep insight into people's social life and religious beliefs. The annual calendar is characterized by a variety of festivals that have both religious and secular significance and often last for generations.

One of the most important religious festivals in Turkey is the Ramadan festival, also known as the Eid al-Fitr (Şeker Bayramı). It marks the end of the fasting month of Ramadan and is a time of joy and coming together for Muslim families. The festival begins with the festive prayer on the morning of the first day and includes visiting relatives and friends, exchanging gifts and sharing sweets.

Another important religious festival is the Feast of Sacrifice (Kurban Bayramı), which commemorates Ibrahim and his will to sacrifice his son Ishmael. During this festival, Muslims traditionally sacrifice an animal and share the meat with the needy and the community. It is a time of reflection and prayer, but also of social interaction and care for others.

In addition to religious festivals, there are also a variety of cultural and national celebrations in Turkey. For example, April 23 is celebrated as "Children's Day" (Ulusal Egemenlik ve Çocuk Bayramı), which celebrates the founding of the Turkish National Assembly in 1920 and the establishment of the Republic of Turkey in 1923. On this day, children are particularly honored and events and festivities take place throughout the country.

May 19 is another important holiday in Turkey, known as "Youth and Sports Day" (Gençlik ve Spor Bayramı), which honors youth and their contribution to the independence movement. This day is celebrated with sporting competitions, parades and cultural events to celebrate youth and strengthen national values.

Traditional customs in Turkey also include the New Year (Yılbaşı), which is celebrated on December 31 and is associated with festive meals, fireworks, and the exchange of gifts. The Turkish New Year is an occasion for family and friends to come together and reflect on the past year and welcome the coming year.

Weddings (Düğün) are also significant celebrations in Turkish culture, often lasting several days and associated with traditional ceremonies, music and dance. Weddings are not only occasions for the bride and groom, but also for families, friends and communities to celebrate and strengthen their bond.

In addition, there are many regional festivals and customs in Turkey that date back to local traditions and history. These festivals can have religious, cultural or seasonal themes and offer insights into the diversity of Turkish culture and way of life.

Overall, customs and festivals play a central role in Turkey's social life and are an expression of cultural identity, cohesion and traditions that have been maintained over generations. They are not only a cause for joy and celebration, but also an important part of the country's social and cultural heritage.

Religion in Turkey: Islam and Diversity

Religion plays an important role in social life in Turkey and is a central aspect of the country's cultural identity. Islam is the predominant religion and shapes the daily life of many Turks in various aspects. About 99% of the population is Muslim, with the majority belonging to the Sunni branch of Islam.

The history of Islam in Turkey dates back to the Ottoman era, when the Ottoman Empire was one of the most significant Islamic empires in history. During this time, Islam developed as a central part of the empire's political and cultural identity, and numerous significant Islamic institutions and buildings were built, including mosques, madrasahs (Islamic schools), and Sufi orders.

Today, Turkey is known for its diversity within Islam, both theologically and spiritually. In addition to Sunni Islam, there are also Shia, Alevi and Sufi traditions that play a significant role in the religious life of some communities. Alevis, a significant religious minority in Turkey, practice a syncretic faith that combines elements of Shiite Islam, Sufism and Turkish folklore.

The Turkish constitution guarantees freedom of religion and the separation of state and religion, although Islam exerts a strong cultural and social influence. The President of Turkey is also traditionally the country's religious leader and is supported by the Directorate of Religious Affairs (Diyanet İşleri Başkanlığı), which is responsible for managing the religious institutions and promoting Islam.

In addition to Islam, there are also small religious minorities in Turkey, including Christians (mainly Orthodox Greeks, Armenians and Syrians), Jews and Baha'is. These religious minorities have historically played a significant role in Turkey's social and cultural life, although their numbers have declined over time.

Religious festivals and customs are important occasions in the Turkish calendar and provide an opportunity for community and the celebration of religious identity. Ramadan, the month of fasting, is a time of reflection and prayer, followed by the Ramadan festival (Şeker Bayramı), which celebrates the end of the month of fasting. The Feast of Sacrifice (Kurban Bayramı) commemorates Ibrahim's willingness to sacrifice and is an occasion for offerings and communal celebrations.

Overall, Turkey's religious diversity reflects its complex history, cultural diversity, and religious tolerance. However, Islam remains the dominant faith in the country and shapes both the personal and public lives of Turks.

Turkey's education system

Turkey's education system is a central pillar of national development and has evolved greatly over time. It includes a wide range of educational institutions ranging from kindergarten to higher education.

The basis of the education system is compulsory primary education, which is mandatory for children aged six to 14. Primary school attendance is free and compulsory, with compulsory schooling until the age of 18. The goal of basic education is to provide students with basic knowledge in subjects such as mathematics, languages, science, and social studies.

After primary education, students have the opportunity to enter secondary schools, including grammar schools (Lise) and vocational schools (Meslek Lisesi). Grammar schools offer a general education programme that prepares students for the higher education entrance qualification, while vocational schools provide practical skills and knowledge in specific occupational fields.

Turkey's education system is highly centralized and is managed by the Ministry of National Education (Milli Eğitim Bakanlığı), which is responsible for curriculum development, teacher training, and school supervision. There are also a growing number of private schools that offer alternative educational offerings for students interested in specialized or international education programs.

Higher education plays an important role in Turkey's education system, and the country has a variety of universities and colleges. The largest and most prestigious universities are located in the big cities such as Istanbul, Ankara, and Izmir. The higher education system offers programs in a variety of disciplines, including engineering, medicine, humanities, natural sciences, and social sciences.

Turkey has made great efforts in recent years to improve educational opportunities and increase the quality of education. Nevertheless, the education system faces challenges such as overcrowding in urban schools, unequal access to educational resources, and the integration of refugee children from neighboring countries.

Overall, Turkey's education system reflects dynamic development and efforts to provide quality education for all citizens in order to support national development goals and strengthen the competitiveness of the economy.

Traditional handicrafts in Turkey

Traditional craftsmanship in Turkey has a rich history and is deeply rooted in the country's cultural identity. Over centuries, Turkish craftsmen and artists have developed a variety of skills and techniques that have often been passed down from generation to generation.

An outstanding example of traditional craftsmanship in Turkey is carpet knotting, especially the world-famous oriental carpets. These rugs are woven by hand and are known for their intricate design, fine detail and vibrant colours. Each rug is unique, often requiring months or even years of work.

Another important craft is ceramic production, which has a long tradition in various regions of Turkey. Iznik ceramics, named after the town of Iznik, are famous for their turquoise patterns and geometric designs, often inspired by nature. These ceramics have been produced since the 15th century and are still popular collector's items today.

The production of copperware is another traditional craft that is widely used in Turkey. Coppersmiths produce ornately decorated pots, bowls, plates and other everyday objects, which are often provided with filigree patterns and engravings. These artisans often use techniques such as hammering, engraving, and patination to create unique pieces.

Wood carving is also an important traditional craft in Turkey, which is used in both architecture and furniture making. Fine carvings are often used in mosques, palaces, and traditional homes to create decorative elements such as door panels, window frames, and pieces of furniture.

Another notable craft is the production of Turkish kilims, flat fabrics traditionally used as flooring or wall hangings. These kilims are woven on a loom and are known for their geometric patterns and vibrant colors that often reflect regional differences.

In addition to these main areas, there are many other traditional crafts in Turkey, including the production of mosaics, jewelry, leather goods, pottery, and more. These crafts are not only an expression of the artistic skills of the craftsmen, but also an important part of Turkish culture and identity. They help preserve the country's history and traditions and are often a significant industry in many Turkish cities and regions.

The Textile Art of Turkey: Carpets and More

Turkey's textile art is known worldwide for its exceptional craftsmanship and rich cultural significance. A central element of this textile art are the famous Turkish carpets, which have played a prominent role for centuries. These rugs are hand-knotted or woven by highly skilled artisans in different regions of the country, with each region cultivating its own traditional patterns, designs, and techniques.

The most famous Turkish carpets are the oriental carpets, which are appreciated for their fine craftsmanship and the use of high-quality materials such as wool, silk and cotton. Each rug is unique and often a work of art in itself, telling stories of culture, history and tradition. Knotting techniques can vary depending on the region and design, with some rugs being made by hand over months or even years.

In addition to carpets, Turkish textile art is also known for its fine silk fabrics, which are often provided with elaborate embroidery and decorations. These silk fabrics are often used for traditional clothing such as caftans and scarves, which are worn both in everyday life and on festive occasions.

Another significant element of Turkish textile art is the hand-woven kilims, flat fabrics that are traditionally used as floor coverings or wall hangings. These kilims are woven on looms and are known for their geometric patterns, vivid colors and robustness. They often reflect regional traditions and artistic expressions.

Turkey is also known for its batik and dyeing techniques, where fabrics are dyed with natural dyes such as indigo and madder to create ornate patterns and designs. These traditional dyeing techniques are often used in combination with other textile techniques to create unique fabrics for clothing, home textiles and crafts.

In addition to artisanal textile production, Turkey has developed a modern textile industry that includes high-tech production processes for clothing, home textiles, and technical textiles. This industry plays a significant role in the Turkish economy and exports products all over the world.

Overall, Turkey's textile art is not only an important economic sector, but also an essential part of the country's cultural identity. It combines traditional craftsmanship with modern innovations, helping to preserve and develop the heritage of Turkish culture.

The Turkish Film Industry

The Turkish film industry has undergone an impressive development over the years and now plays a significant role in international cinema. The beginnings of Turkish cinema date back to the early 1910s, when the first silent films were produced. The first Turkish feature film, "Arap Bedii", was produced in 1914 by Şehzade Abdülmecid Efendi.

In the 1950s and 1960s, Turkish cinema experienced a heyday known as the golden age of Turkish cinema. Films from this era, especially melodramas and historical dramas, shaped the country's film landscape and also gained international recognition at film festivals.

In the 1970s, Turkish cinema continued to develop, with the genre of "Yeşilçam cinema" (after the street name in Istanbul, where many film studios were located) being particularly formative. These films covered a variety of topics, including love stories, social issues, and action movies. Actors such as Türkan Şoray, Kadir İnanır and Cüneyt Arkın became national stars and left a lasting mark on Turkey's pop culture.

In recent decades, the Turkish film industry has undergone modernization and has become more competitive internationally. New generations of directors and producers have introduced new themes and narrative styles that are attracting attention both in Turkey and abroad. In particular, the emergence of independent filmmakers has led to a diversity of voices and stories that enrich modern Turkish cinema.

An important milestone for Turkish cinema was the establishment of the Istanbul International Film Festival in 1982, which became a significant venue for the presentation of Turkish and international films. This event has helped to raise the profile of Turkish cinema in a global context and to promote cooperation between Turkish and foreign filmmakers.

Today, Turkey is an important production location for films and television series. Istanbul and other cities offer modern film studios and facilities that are used for both domestic and international productions. Turkish series, especially in the genre of dramas and soap operas, have also found a large following outside of Turkey, especially in the countries of the Middle East and Europe.

However, the Turkish film industry also faces challenges, including financial constraints, legal frameworks, and cultural debates. Nevertheless, it remains a dynamic and innovative industry that constantly produces new talent and expresses Turkey's rich cultural diversity on the screen.

Sports and Leisure in Turkey

Sports and leisure play a significant role in Turkey's everyday life and reflect the diversity of the country's cultural, geographical, and climatic conditions. Football is undoubtedly the most popular sport in Turkey and enjoys a passionate following. The Süper Lig is the highest football league in the country, with prestigious clubs such as Galatasaray, Fenerbahçe and Beşiktaş competing for the championship.

In addition to football, basketball, volleyball, handball and wrestling are also popular sports. The Turkish basketball league (Basketbol Süper Ligi) is also highly regarded and has produced national stars who are also internationally successful. In volleyball, the Turkish women's national team is one of the top teams in the world.

Traditional Turkish martial arts such as wrestling and karate have deep historical roots and are actively practiced. Wrestlers like Hamza Yerlikaya have won medals at the Olympics and World Championships and contribute to the popularity of this sport. Karate, especially in its traditional form of Shotokan, is valued by many Turks as a cultural heritage and is practiced by numerous clubs and schools throughout the country.

Turkey also offers ideal conditions for water sports such as sailing, windsurfing and diving. The country's coastline on the Mediterranean, the Aegean Sea and the Black Sea offers numerous opportunities for water sports enthusiasts. Places like Bodrum, Antalya, and İzmir are known for their marinas and sailing regattas, while the marine life along the coast is rich in marine life forms.

For hikers and nature lovers, Turkey offers an impressive landscape with numerous hiking and trekking routes. Cappadocia, with its bizarre rock formations and caves, is a hiker's paradise, while the Lycian Way along the Lycian coast is considered one of the most beautiful long-distance hiking trails in the world.

In winter, Turkey's mountains attract skiers and snowboarders. The ski resorts of Uludağ near Bursa, Palandöken near Erzurum and Kartalkaya near Bolu offer first-class slopes and facilities for winter sports. These regions attract both national and international visitors every year who want to enjoy skiing and snowboarding in a scenic setting.

In addition to these traditional sports, there is also a growing popularity in Turkey for modern leisure activities such as gyms, spinning classes and yoga. Major cities such as Istanbul and

Ankara offer a variety of leisure facilities, including parks, fitness clubs, and sports centers that cater to the needs of residents and visitors alike.

In conclusion, sports and leisure in Turkey are not only an important part of the country's culture and identity, but also provide opportunities for physical activities and recreation in a diverse and scenic environment.

Tourism in Turkey: An industry in transition

Tourism in Turkey has played a turbulent history and a significant economic role that has developed over many decades. Beginning in the 1950s, Turkey experienced a steady increase in the number of visitors, especially from European countries discovering the country's rich culture, historical sites, and natural beauty.

In the 1970s and 1980s, tourism in Turkey reached its peak with strong infrastructure development and a variety of new hotels, resorts, and tourist services. The focus was on the coastal regions on the Mediterranean and the Aegean Sea, as well as on historic cities such as Istanbul, Ankara and Ephesus, which became the main attractions for visitors.

The advent of all-inclusive resorts in coastal cities such as Antalya and Bodrum shaped Turkey's tourist offer, attracting millions of holidaymakers who wanted to enjoy the country's sun, sea and hospitable atmosphere. The Turkish government actively supported the development of the tourism sector by promoting investment in infrastructure and the promotion of the country's cultural heritage.

In the 1990s and at the beginning of the 21st century, Turkish tourism experienced both ups and downs. Political instability in the region, economic crises and security concerns after various terrorist attacks temporarily affected the influx of tourists. Nevertheless, the sector recovered through targeted marketing measures, improved safety precautions and the diversification of the tourist offer.

Cultural tourism plays a central role in Turkey's tourism strategy, as the country has a rich historical and cultural heritage. UNESCO World Heritage Sites such as Pamukkale, Goreme National Park, and Istanbul's Old Town attract visitors from all over the world. In addition, archaeological sites such as Troy, Pergamon, and Hierapolis offer insights into Anatolia's ancient history and contribute to Turkey's appeal as a cultural destination.

In addition to cultural tourism, ecotourism has established itself as a growing sector, attracting visitors to remote regions such as the Black Sea region and Cappadocia, where they can experience Turkey's natural beauty and ecological diversity. Activities such as hiking, rafting, bird watching and eco-lodges contribute to the sustainable development of the tourism sector.

In recent years, Turkey has also increased its investment in health tourism, especially in thermal baths and wellness centers in cities such as Afyon and Bursa, which are known for their healing thermal springs. Medical tourism, which provides high-quality healthcare services at affordable prices, has also gained prominence.

Digital transformation has further driven Turkish tourism, as online platforms and social media play a crucial role in marketing destinations and interacting with travelers. Turkey strives to strengthen its reputation as a versatile and hospitable destination while promoting the sustainable development of the tourism sector in order to benefit from the economic and social benefits of tourism in the long term.

Turkey's famous thermal springs

Turkey is known for its rich thermal spring landscape, which has attracted visitors from all over the world for centuries. These natural hot springs are spread throughout the country, from the Aegean Sea to the Sea of Marmara to the Black Sea coast and the interior of Anatolia. Turkey's thermal springs are not only places of relaxation and recreation, but also have a long history as healing springs and are embedded in the country's cultural and historical identity.

Afyonkarahisar, a city in western Turkey, is famous for its thermal springs and is often referred to as the "home of thermal springs." The city is rich in natural mineral springs, the water of which is prized for its health benefits. Particularly well-known are the thermal baths of Afyon, where visitors can enjoy the beneficial properties of the mineral springs in a relaxing environment.

Another prominent thermal center is Pamukkale in southwestern Turkey. This is where the famous "Cotton Castle" is formed, a unique formation of limestone terraces and thermal pools created by the hot spring water. Pamukkale is not only a UNESCO World Heritage Site, but also a significant destination for health tourism, where visitors can bathe in the natural thermal pools and experience the healing properties of the water.

Bursa, a city at the foot of the Uludağ Mountains, is also known for its thermal springs. Bursa's thermal springs have been known since Byzantine times and attract both locals and international visitors. The thermal baths such as Çekirge are famous for their healing properties and are visited by people seeking relief from various health ailments.

The region around Lake Çıldır in northeastern Turkey is also home to thermal springs, which are a popular choice for travelers who want to enjoy the tranquility and natural beauty of the Turkish countryside due to their secluded location and natural surroundings.

Turkey has also invested in modern thermal and spa facilities that provide high-quality health and wellness services in recent years. These facilities combine traditional healing methods with modern therapies and technologies to meet the needs of a discerning global audience.

Turkey's thermal springs are therefore not only an important cultural heritage, but also an important economic factor in the field of health tourism. They offer visitors the chance to experience Turkey's natural beauty while benefiting from the health benefits of the thermal springs.

Wellness and Health Tourism in Turkey

Wellness and health tourism have a long tradition in Turkey and play a significant role in the country's tourism sector. Turkey is known for its rich thermal spring landscape, which has attracted visitors seeking relaxation and healing for centuries. The thermal baths and spas in cities such as Afyonkarahisar, Pamukkale, Bursa, and other places offer a variety of health and wellness services based on natural resources such as mineral water and mud.

Afyonkarahisar, often referred to as the "Home of the Hot Springs", is a prominent health tourism center in Turkey. The city is known for its numerous thermal baths, which are prized for their healing properties. Visitors can relax in natural thermal springs and benefit from the minerals in the water, which are known for their health benefits.

Pamukkale in southwestern Turkey is another famous destination for wellness and health tourism. The "Cotton Castle" of Pamukkale is a UNESCO World Heritage Site and is known for its terraced limestone pools created by the hot spring water. Visitors can not only admire the unique landscape, but also bathe in the thermal pools and enjoy the healing properties of the water.

Bursa, a historic city at the foot of the Uludağ Mountains, also offers a rich thermal spring landscape. The thermal baths of Bursa, such as the one in Çekirge, have been known since the Byzantine period and are visited by people seeking relief from various health ailments. The city is also known for its traditional silk production and historic architecture, making it an attractive destination for wellness travelers interested in culture.

Turkey has invested in modern wellness and spa facilities that offer a wide range of healthcare services in recent years. These facilities combine traditional healing methods with modern therapies and technologies to meet the needs of a global audience. They offer weight loss programs, detoxification, stress relief, anti-aging treatments, and much more, often performed in a relaxing and luxurious environment.

Health tourism in Turkey includes not only thermal springs and spas, but also medical services such as cosmetic surgery, dental treatments, and eye surgeries, which are offered at attractive prices and with high-quality medical care. Turkey is increasingly positioning itself as a leading destination for health and wellness travel, attracting millions of visitors each year who want to enjoy the country's natural beauties while increasing their well-being.

The main tourist attractions

Turkey is rich in historical and cultural attractions that attract visitors from all over the world. One of the most famous tourist attractions is undoubtedly Istanbul, the fascinating city that lies on two continents. Here, visitors can tour the majestic Hagia Sophia, which was once a church, then a mosque, and now a museum. The nearby Topkapı Palace with its magnificent gardens and treasures from the Ottoman Empire also attracts numerous tourists.

On the Aegean coast rises the ancient city of Ephesus, once a major metropolis of the Roman Empire, now a fascinating archaeological site. The well-preserved Library of Celsus and the impressive theater are just a few of the highlights that await visitors here.

Pamukkale, the "Cotton Castle", is known for its calcareous terraced pools and thermal springs, which have attracted people seeking healing and relaxation for centuries. The gleaming white pools and ancient ruins of the Greco-Roman city of Hierapolis make this place a UNESCO World Heritage Site.

The Cappadocia region, famous for its unique landscape of fairy chimneys and underground cities, offers not only spectacular views but also a rich cultural heritage. Hot air balloon rides over the bizarre rock formations are particularly popular here.

Antalya on the Turkish Riviera attracts with beautiful beaches and ancient ruins such as the old town of Side and the ancient theater of Aspendos. The region is also known for its luxurious resorts and the clear, blue waters of the Mediterranean.

Not to forget the Goreme National Park in Cappadocia, famous for its cave churches with Byzantine frescoes. These historic caves, which once served as Christian sanctuaries, are also a UNESCO World Heritage Site and attract visitors from all over the world.

Turkey offers a variety of attractions to suit all tastes and interests, be it ancient cities, impressive landscapes, religious monuments, or modern cities with vibrant life. Each region of the country holds unique treasures waiting to be discovered, making Turkey an unforgettable destination for culture and history buffs as well as those seeking relaxation.

Turkey for Adventurers: Trekking and Mountaineering

Turkey offers adventurers and nature lovers a variety of opportunities for trekking and mountaineering in different regions of the country. One of the outstanding regions is undoubtedly the Taurus Mountains in the southern part of Anatolia. This majestic mountain range stretches for hundreds of kilometers and offers a variety of hiking and climbing routes suitable for both beginners and experienced mountaineers.

In the Taurus Mountains there are numerous peaks over 3000 meters high, including the highest mountain in Turkey, Mount Ararat, with its 5137 meters. Ararat is not only a geographical icon, but also a spiritual and historical site that poses a challenge for mountaineers who want to climb the summit.

The region around Mount Ararat also offers spectacular landscapes with deep gorges, green valleys and alpine lakes that will make the heart of any adventurer beat faster. However, climbing Mount Ararat requires some preparation and acclimatization due to its altitude and alpine conditions.

For trekking enthusiasts, the famous Lycian Way, which runs along the Lycian coast in southwestern Turkey, is a good choice. This long-distance hiking trail stretches for about 500 kilometers and leads through an impressive landscape of coastal cliffs, pine forests and ancient ruins. The Lycian Way is known for its variety of terrain and the opportunity to enjoy breathtaking views of the turquoise Mediterranean Sea.

Another popular region for trekking is Cappadocia, which is not only known for its fairy chimneys, but also for its numerous hiking trails through valleys, gorges, and historic villages. Hikers can explore the unique landscape, discovering cave churches, underground cities, and picturesque vineyards along the way.

In addition to these well-known regions, there are many other places in Turkey that are ideal for trekking and mountaineering. The eastern regions of Anatolia, for example, offer challenging routes through the fascinating landscapes of Lake Van and the Nemrut Mountains. Here, adventurers can not only test their physical limits, but also delve deep into the culture and history of Turkey.

Turkey is thus not only a place for sun worshippers and culture lovers, but also a paradise for adventurers who are attracted by the diversity of landscapes and the challenge of the mountains. With its rich natural diversity and historical depth, Turkey offers an unparalleled backdrop for an unforgettable adventure in the heart of Anatolia.

Sailing and water sports in Turkey

Turkey is a paradise for sailors and water sports enthusiasts, thanks to its long coastline that includes both the Mediterranean Sea and the Aegean Sea. Sailing is one of the most popular activities along the Turkish coast, attracting sailors from all over the world. Turkey has numerous well-equipped marinas and marinas that provide an ideal base for sailing adventures.

The Aegean Sea offers particularly good sailing conditions with stable winds and picturesque islands to explore. The region around Bodrum, Marmaris and Fethiye is particularly popular with sailors who want to experience the beauty of the Turkish coast. These areas are known for their sheltered bays, crystal clear waters, and ancient ruins that combine a sailing experience with cultural discoveries.

In the Mediterranean, Turkey attracts with its diverse sailing routes along the coast of the Turkish Riviera. Cities such as Antalya and Alanya offer not only beautiful beaches, but also opportunities for water sports such as windsurfing, kitesurfing, and jet skiing. The Turkish Riviera is also known for its luxury yachts, which are anchored here during the summer season.

For adventure seekers and experienced sailors, Turkey also offers the opportunity for offshore adventures. The Dardanelles and Bosphorus are important sea routes that connect the Black Sea to the Mediterranean Sea and pose a challenge for sailors who want to cross the waterways.

In addition to sailing, Turkey is also a popular destination for divers. The coasts offer rich marine life with coral reefs, sunken shipwrecks, and a variety of marine life. Diving schools and diving centers along the coast offer courses for beginners as well as guided dives to the best dive sites in the region.

Water sports such as water skiing, parasailing and banana boating are also widely available in the tourist coastal resorts and offer fun for the whole family. Turkey has established itself as a versatile water sports destination that has something to offer for both adventurers and those seeking relaxation.

Overall, the Turkish coast is a magnet for water sports lovers from all over the world who want to enjoy the variety of activities and the beauty of the coast. With its mild climate, rich history, and breathtaking landscapes, Turkey is an unparalleled destination for sailors and water sports enthusiasts alike.

Tips for travelers in Turkey

For travelers who want to visit Turkey, there are a variety of practical tips to make their trip enjoyable and smooth. First of all, it is important to respect the cultural customs of the country. Turkey is a predominantly Muslim nation, so one should wear appropriate clothing, especially when visiting religious sites such as mosques. Women are often advised to bring a headscarf to cover their heads.

Another important aspect is the currency. The official currency of Turkey is the Turkish lira (TRY). It is advisable to exchange some lira for cash, as not all shops and restaurants accept credit cards, especially outside the tourist areas.

Turkey offers a variety of accommodation options, from luxury hotels to hostels and vacation rentals. It is advisable to book accommodation in advance, especially during the high season in summer.

In terms of safety, travelers should be aware that Turkey is a safe country to visit, but as everywhere else in the world, tourists should observe basic safety measures. It is recommended not to show valuables openly and to take good care of your personal belongings.

Turkey has a well-developed transport network that allows travelers to explore the country comfortably. Public transportation in major cities such as

Istanbul, Ankara, and Izmir is reliable and affordable. For longer distances, long-distance buses and trains are available, which run regularly between the cities.

Turkish cuisine is known worldwide for its variety and taste. A visit to local restaurants and cafes is a must to try traditional dishes such as kebab, meze and baklava. It is also recommended not to drink the tap water, but instead consume bottled water to avoid possible health problems.

Culturally interested travelers can explore Turkey's rich history and impressive sights, including ancient ruins, Ottoman palaces, and UNESCO World Heritage Sites. It's worth setting aside some time to visit these historic sites and consider taking a guided tour to learn more about the history and significance of these places.

After all, Turkey is known for its hospitality and friendliness towards visitors. A few basic knowledge of Turkish can be helpful, but most people in tourist areas also speak English or German. However, a smile and a respectful attitude often go further than words.

Overall, Turkey offers a fascinating mix of history, culture, nature, and hospitality that will delight any traveler. By taking these practical tips into account, you can enjoy your trip to Turkey to the fullest.

Closing remarks

This book on Turkey offers a comprehensive overview of the many aspects of this fascinating country. From rich history to vibrant culture, from breathtaking nature to hospitable society, Turkey is undoubtedly a country of contrasts and beauty.

In previous chapters, we've explored the geography of Turkey, from the shores of the Mediterranean Sea to the majestic mountains of Anatolia. We have shed light on the rich history of the country, from ancient civilizations to the modern Republic of Turkey. The cultural diversity and traditions of Turkey were highlighted, from the customs and festivals to the modern art scene and the living musical tradition.

Special attention was paid to the cities and regions of Turkey, starting with the vibrant metropolis of Istanbul and the historic capital Ankara to the idyllic coastal cities such as Izmir and Antalya. We explored the ancient wonders of Ephesus and Pamukkale, admired the fairytale landscape of Cappadocia, and enjoyed the natural beauty of the Black Sea region and the Lycian coast.

The wildlife and natural treasures of Turkey were presented as well as the culinary delights, starting with the famous Turkish carpets and ending with the delicious dishes of Turkish cuisine. We have dealt with Turkey's education system, modern economic life and the dynamic art scene.

In addition, we took a look at Turkey's religious and social context, especially Islam and the country's cultural diversity. Turkey's role in global politics and business was highlighted, as well as its importance as a major tourist destination.

In conclusion, I would like to emphasize that Turkey is not only a country of history and nature, but also a country of hospitality and openness. The Turks are proud of their rich cultural heritage and warmly welcome visitors from all over the world.

This book is not only intended to give you a comprehensive understanding of Turkey, but also to arouse your curiosity to discover this multifaceted country for yourself. May your trip through Turkey be full of unforgettable experiences and enriching encounters.

Made in the USA
Las Vegas, NV
26 May 2025

22748783R00066